What We Saw in the School Garden

By Stan Cullimore

Contents

Section 1

Ladybirds   2

Ants   8

Section 2

Bees   12

Spiders   18

Section 3

Caterpillars and Butterflies   22

Grasshoppers   28

Longman

Ladybirds

When we went into the school garden we saw a ladybird.

It was on a leaf.

It had a black head.

It had a red body.

It had black spots on its back.

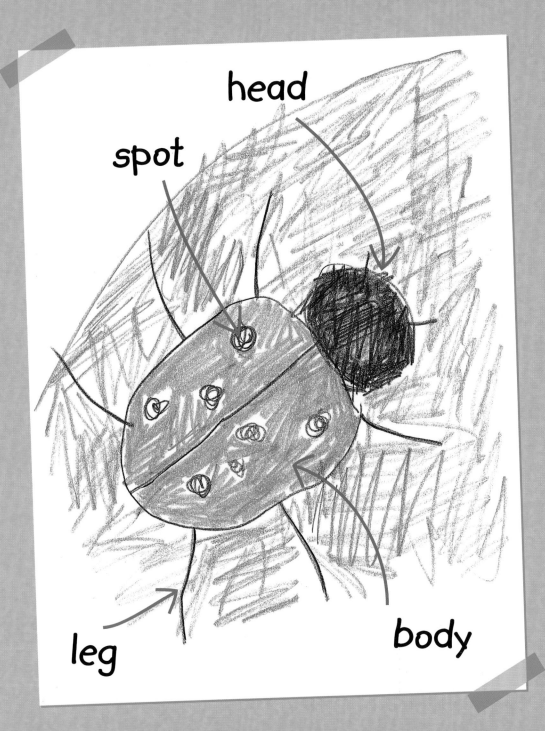

head

spot

leg

body

4

I put my hand by the leaf.
The ladybird walked onto my hand.
It tickled.

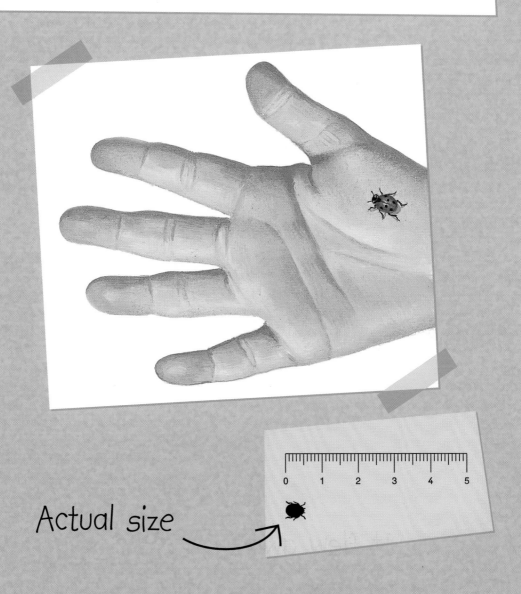

Actual size

I moved my hand.
The ladybird opened its wings.

It flew away.

Ladybird facts:

- They eat greenfly.

- They lay their eggs on leaves.

- They can live for about two years.

We saw some ants in the garden.

They were on the ground.

The ants were very small.

head   leg   body

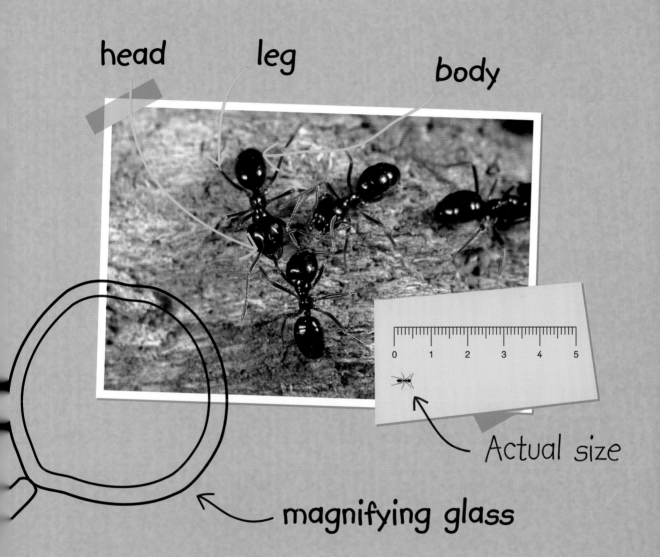

Actual size

magnifying glass

We used a magnifying glass to look at them.

Ants have six legs.
They can run very fast.

We saw them run into a hole.

Ant facts:

- Ants live in nests under the ground.

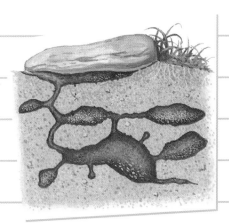

- Some ants can fly.

- Red ants can bite you. It stings!

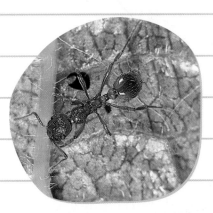

Bees

When we went into the school garden we saw a bee.

0 1 2 3 4 5

Actual size

It was on a flower.

The bee went inside another flower.
When it came out it had yellow
powder on its back legs.
Our teacher told us that it was pollen.

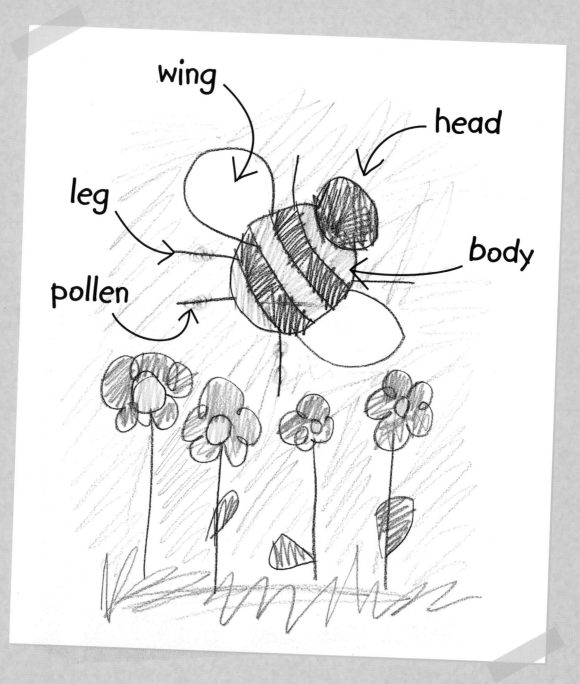

wing

head

leg

body

pollen

14

We watched the bee fly to another bush. It made a buzzing sound when it flew.

pollen

15

Bees live in beehives.
There are thousands of bees in each beehive.

Bee facts:

- Most bees live for about a year.

- Bees use nectar to make honey.

- Bees can sting you. So be careful!

Spiders

We saw a spider's web in the school garden.
There was a spider sitting in the middle of it.

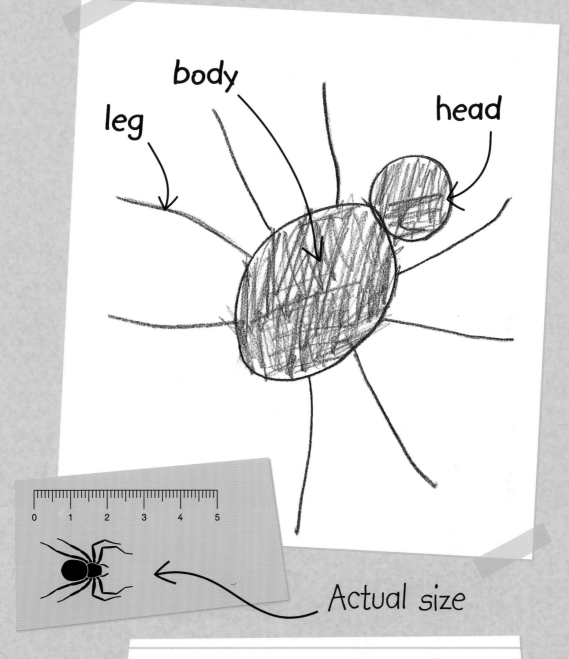

leg

body

head

Actual size

The spider had eight legs –
I counted them all!

A fly got stuck in the web. The spider grabbed the fly before it could get away.

Spider facts:

- Spiders eat flies.

- Some spiders spin a new web every day!

- Spiders spin silk. The silk from a spider is stronger than steel. Some spiders' silk is actually bullet-proof!

Caterpillars and Butterflies

We saw a caterpillar in the school garden.
It was green and it had hairs sticking out along its back.

It had lots of legs.
We watched it crawl along a twig.

It had a funny
way of moving.

Like this!

Our teacher told us that when caterpillars are ready they spin a cocoon.
They stay inside it for a few weeks.

cocoon

When the caterpillar comes out of the cocoon it has changed.

It has turned into a butterfly.

Actual size

We saw a butterfly in the school garden.
It was on a flower.
It was sucking nectar out of the flower.

Butterfly facts:

- Butterflies lay eggs on leaves.

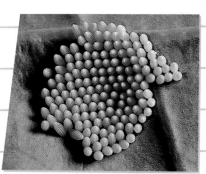

- Butterflies have very long tongues.

- There are lots of different sorts of butterflies.

- Most butterflies only live for a few months.

Grasshoppers

When we were in the school garden we heard a chirruping sound coming from the grass.
We saw a grasshopper.
It was the grasshopper that was making the noise!

When I tried to catch it in my hands it jumped away.
It jumped very quickly.

Actual size

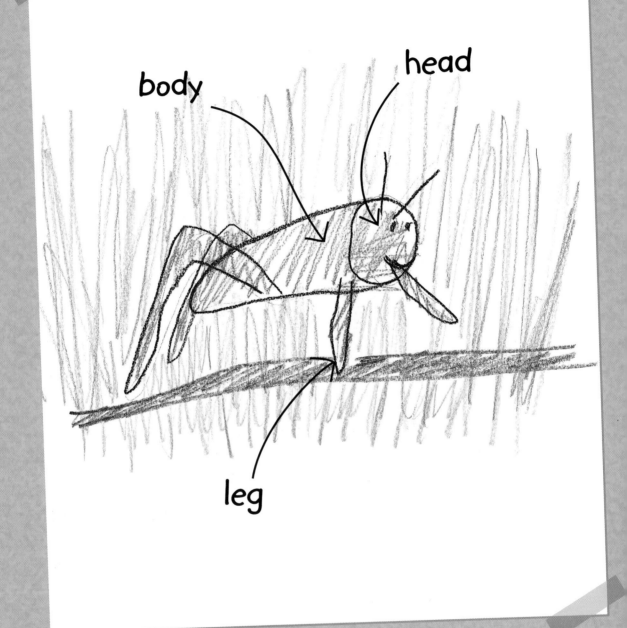

body

head

leg

Grasshopper facts:

- Grasshoppers eat leaves.

- Grasshoppers can jump 20 times their own length!

- Some grasshoppers have wings and can fly.

- Grasshoppers make the chirruping sound by rubbing their back legs on their bodies.

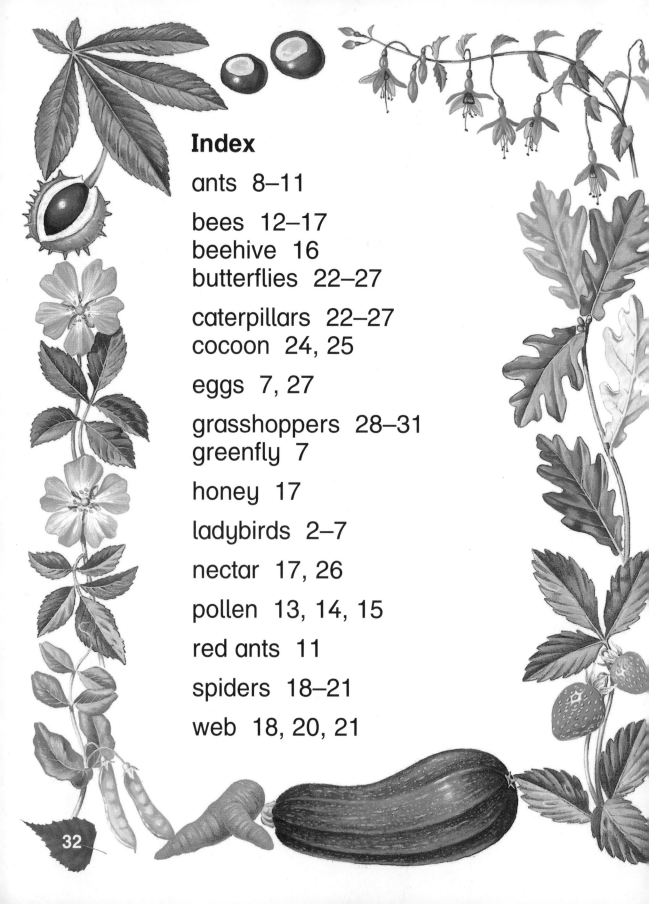

Index

ants 8–11

bees 12–17
beehive 16
butterflies 22–27

caterpillars 22–27
cocoon 24, 25

eggs 7, 27

grasshoppers 28–31
greenfly 7

honey 17

ladybirds 2–7

nectar 17, 26

pollen 13, 14, 15

red ants 11

spiders 18–21

web 18, 20, 21